Even Our Friendship Was Illegal

COE STUDENTS CONFRONT MISSISSIPPI SEGREGATION IN 1962

**Edited by
Fritze Roberts '99**

With Contributions from:

Vicki Burroughs Bixler '62
Dale Ely '63
Philip K. Ensley '65
Judith Lamparek Lanum '64
Sally Fels Meyers '64
Dorothy McCarter Quiggin '62
William H. Schalk '65
Jean Johnson Sidner '63

Coe Review Press
CEDAR RAPIDS, IA

Roberts/Coe College
1220 1st Ave, NE
Cedar Rapids, IA 52402
www.coe.edu

Book Layout ©2013 BookDesignTemplates.com

Ordering Information:
Quantity sales. Special discounts are available on quantity purchases by corporations, associations, and others. For details, contact the Jean Johnson, Office of Alumni, at the address above.

Even Our Friendship was Illegal: Coe Students Confront Mississippi Segregation in 1962/ Fritze Roberts. —1st ed.
ISBN 978-1-5391-3898-3

Contents

Coe College Service Projects 1

The Decision to Go to Tougaloo 5

Showing Up is Half the Battle 15

    The Journey to Tougaloo 16

    Arrival at the Tougaloo Campus 19

Observing Racism and Inequality 27

    Separate, Not Equal 30

    Under-funded Public Schools 31

    Interviewing Mississippi Governor Ross Barnett 33

    Getting to Know the Tougaloo Students 34

    Segregation at the Airport 36

    The White Citizens Council 37

    Visit to Rural Areas Near Tougaloo 38

    Cultural Laws of Racism 42

Meeting Civil Rights Leaders 43

Medgar Evers...43

James Meredith and Constance Baker Motley..44

Dr. Ernst Borinski..45

Attorney Bill Higgs...49

Coe Students Harassed and Arrested..51

Social Events...61

Life After Tougaloo and Coe..65

Recommended Reading..73

All ages...73

Juvenile fiction..73

Related links:..75

Dr. Ernst Borinski...75

Coe College...75

Dedicated to the Memory of
The Rev. Dr. John C. Walker, B.A., B.D., M. Div., Ph.D.
College Chaplain, 1959 – 1969
Professor of Philosophy and Religion, 1959 – 1977

To Jane + Brian,

It was wonderful meeting and sharing the evening with you. I hope you enjoy reading about my adventures in Mississippi in 1962.

With love,

Bill Schall

Acknowledgements

This collection of stories honors our leaders: Dr. John Walker, Coe's Chaplain and project organizer, and Dr. Ernst Borinski, Professor of Sociology and German, who was our teacher and host at Tougaloo College. Their skills and delightful personalities were key to our overall experience and to the success of the project.

We remember Gini Knight '65, a member of our group who has since passed away. Gini approached everything with enthusiasm. Her warmth and unforgettable smile were much appreciated – as were her notes on our daily activities that helped in compiling our initial account of the project.

We remember with thanks the openness and generosity of the Tougaloo students and staff, who took the time to get to know us and shared some of themselves in the process.

We are grateful for the people who welcomed us to their church services, meetings, homes, offices, and community programs, and those community leaders who came to the campus to share their insights and experiences in learning sessions with us.

We would also like to acknowledge and applaud the interest and support of Coe's students, faculty, and administration - past and present - who helped make the project possible, and who welcomed us back 50-plus years later to speak of our experiences.

That "welcome back" and this written record were facilitated by the Alumni Office and Director Jean Johnson. Thank you, Jean - for your enthusiastic support and encouragement, for your energy and patience, and for your creativity and resourcefulness. We couldn't have done it without you.

CHAPTER 1

Coe College Service Projects

The Summer Service Projects offered to Coe College students in the 1960s were wonderful opportunities to experience diverse cultures outside of Iowa. I was fortunate to participate in the Tougaloo Project and also the Puerto Rico Project. These adventures were highlights of my Coe College education.

The summer in Tougaloo, Mississippi was in a historic time when cultures were being challenged to change, when America and her black citizens needed to move forward and claim all their rights as Americans. We were in Mississippi to observe, learn, and find a way to help that process.

It has been more than 50 years, and we are still working toward and yearning for a world where all peoples can live in harmony together. This was Dr. Martin Luther King's quest, and so it has been mine. Not in any grand or notable way, but through prayerful thoughts and actions, "to brighten my own little corner of the world."

The Tougaloo experiences taught us how to judge a person not by the color of his skin, or by economic status, or by religion – but by the content of his or her mind and heart, and by the resulting actions. It is my prayer that my actions and thoughts have helped my community, my church, my children, and my grandchildren to treat all in their "corner of the world" with love, respect, and equality.

Judith Lamparek Lanum '64

I've often thought about and appreciated the work Dr. John Walker did in organizing the various summer service projects during my time at Coe: '60 to the Indian Reservation in North Dakota, '61 with the Quakers in Mexico, '62 study groups to Tougaloo, and '63 Puerto Rico. Now, as a "maturing adult," I can only imagine Dr. Walker's planning, organization, coordination, making contacts, selling the concept to Coe's administration, and "herding" twelve students safely into and out of Mississippi in the summer of 1962...all while knowing what was beginning to happen in the South. What an educational opportunity he provided for all of us.

Dale Ely '63

SEATED: Vicki Burroughs, Rosalee Sutton, Dr. Walker, Jean Johnson, and Dottie McCarter. STANDING: Virginia Knight, Sally Fels, Philip Ensley, Bill Schalk, Bob Young, Dale Ely, and Judy Lamparek.

Figure 1: An image from the Coe Acorn depicting participants in the Tougaloo trip with Dr. Walker. Not pictured: Tom Palmberg, Carol Hackenholz.

CHAPTER 2

The Decision to Go to Tougaloo

The rear view mirror gets a little hazy looking back to the summer of 1962 and my participation in Coe's summer service project in Mississippi. The trip made a significant impression on my life later. I don't recall it made that much of an impact upon my return to Coe during the following year. It was an intensive educational experience in Mississippi, but sadly, thinking back, I don't recall I, or we, did that much except to briefly share the experience with classmates, and then life as a college student in Iowa in 1962-1963 went on as before. Civil rights, segregation, and the daily lives of black people were "a problem" in the South, but were not yet resonating as a concern or movement on campus or in our lives. I read about it, but it was "down there" and did not impact my life at college or in my home town. Looking back now, that's a sad commentary on what we as students and a nation were thinking and doing, or better said, not doing.

Thinking about the project now, it was a number of years until I began to fully appreciate the experience and incorporate some of the learning into my life and career. I think a lot of the delay had to do with where and how I grew up, other interests and endeavors after college, and of course, a later touch of maturity, experience, and reflection.

I was raised in a small town of approximately 7,000 in central Illinois. The primary sources of income were farming, employment at a small factory, and coal mining. My parents grew up on farms in Missouri and Iowa, living through the hard times of the Depression and World War II. My father was a coal miner; my mother was a homemaker and did some substitute teaching and practical nursing. I was aware that things in our home were often "tight," but my brother and I had a great childhood. I didn't really think about the religious and ethnic makeup of our community until years later. I remember only one black student four years older in our high school, wasn't aware of any Jewish families, nor heard any foreign language spoken. Looking back, it was a sheltered white community in which to grow up. I left for college with a pretty narrow view of the world outside of small-town rural America.

My world began to expand when I entered Coe in 1959. My awareness and interest in civil rights and segregation was minimal at best. I was focused on my studies and worked to pay for my education. With the beginning of the lunch counter sit-ins in the summer of 1960, followed by the Freedom Riders in the summer of 1961, conversations about the civil rights protests were in the news and slowly began on campus, but were not major topics of discussion as I recall.

In the spring of 1961, Dr. Adam Beittel, President of Tougaloo Southern Christian College, spoke at one of Coe's convocations. He invited our College Chaplain, Dr. John Walker, to organize the third Coe Summer Service Project, 1962, to go to Tougaloo near Jackson, Mississippi, to work and study the culture and environment in Mississippi. Based on my background, I thought this would be an educational opportunity. I applied, was accepted, and it was.

Dale Ely '63

RELIGION IN LIFE WEEK SPEAKER . . .

Dr. A. D. Beittel

Dr. A. D. Beittel, President of Tougaloo Southern Christian College, Tougaloo, Mississippi, graduated from Findlay College, Ohio. He received his master's degree at Oberlin College, and his bachelor of divinity and doctor of philosophy degrees at the University of Chicago. He is a former chairman of the Alabama Division of the Southern Regional Council, former vice president of the Association of Colleges and Secondary Schools for Negroes. He now serves as national secretary of the United Negro College Fund.

Dr. Beittel, a Congregational minister, taught at Earlham and Guilford Colleges and served as dean of the chapel at Beloit College from 1953 to 1960. "During this time the chapel was filled every evening, even though the chapels were voluntary," Dr. Richard Taylor relates.

Dr. Beittel is also a member of the Board of the Southern Regional Council and is very active in organizing interracial work in North Carolina and Alabama.

Figure 2: The biography of Dr. Beittel that appeared in the program of the 1961 Coe Convocation that featured him as a speaker.

In the Fall of 1961, I sat in the very last row of the balcony of the Sinclair Memorial Chapel to hear Dr. Martin Luther King speak to the student body at Coe College. To say that I was naïve is an understatement. I was 19 years old and in my second year at Coe. Shortly after his visit, I was invited by Dr. Walker, college chaplain, to join the group from Coe to visit Tougaloo College in Mississippi during June of 1962. I had served on the Coe Christian Council with Dr. Walker and he must have thought that the experience would enlighten my sheltered life.

I grew up as a child of the Amana Colonies with a very limited understanding of what we referred to as the "outside world." I was one of 25 students that graduated from Amana High School in 1960 and there was no one in the entire student body that wasn't white, and didn't have roots in Amana, or at least Iowa County.

The events of the early '60s and how they would affect the simple world I understood had already raised my awareness. The horrible burnings, beatings, and imprisonments of the Freedom Riders shocked the consciousness of all of us. Uninformed as we were, we could never have imagined that our journey would take place in the middle of and before the burning of Mississippi with the entrance of James Meredith as the first black student at Ole Miss.

Sally Fels Meyers '64

Figure 3: A page from the 1963 Coe Acorn featuring a photo of Dr. Martin Luther King, Jr. when he spoke at Coe in 1961.

I remember that, following my freshman year at Coe, I was to begin a summer field work study program at the Associated Colleges of the Midwest's (ACM) Wilderness Field Station outside of Ely, Minnesota in late June 1962. This was a longtime dream of Professor and Biology Department head Dr. Robert V. Drexler and 1962 was to be the inaugural summer for this program. But there was a three week hiatus from the end of the second semester and when I was to be in Ely. My plan was to stay in Greene Hall, the upper class men's dormitory, and work in the Voorhees Hall campus cafeteria washing pots and pans until time to board a bus for Ely.

An announcement had come out in the *Coe Cosmos* describing a summer service project in Mississippi. It was an offshoot from a visit by a campus guest speaker, the president of the historically black college, Tougaloo Southern Christian College, in Jackson, Mississippi. The project was to coincidently take place following the end of the second semester and before I would need to be in Minnesota.

The program was designed to study race relations, an emerging issue of the times. For me to be considered for the project I was required to write an essay on why I wished to become a participant. I decided to write about memories of my grade school years growing up in Virginia.

I do not remember the details in my essay but I do recall writing about past experiences and questions I had from those earlier years regarding race, and that perhaps this project might provide some answers. I had attended grades one through eight in segregated schools. We lived on a county road and my sister, two brothers, and I were bused to school.

In time I had a bicycle newspaper delivery route. The asphalt road we lived on turned into gravel and dirt about a half a mile down from our house, and at the end of that road was what everybody called "the colored section." I was not allowed to deliver papers nor allowed to solicit new subscriptions there.

Women from the black community would perform domestic work in the homes of the "white community" including our home. Occasionally we saw black kids as they rode their bikes through the white neighborhood. Every kid in those days had a bicycle. How fast you could ride became part of your reputation. I was fast, and could make skid turns on a dime.

The black kids had a different character to their bikes, sort of beat up, stripped down, and chopped. There were no front or rear fenders, the seats were raised, handle bars lowered, the struts to the wheel hubs had clothes pins holding playing cards that made a buzzing sound against the spokes as they flew by. They were lean kids, rode like the wind, much faster than I, laying low on the handle bars, shirts open, shirt tails flapping in the breeze, taking long drags on cigarettes. I never met any of those kids, and in many ways for us it was as though they did not exist. But when I saw them ride through I remember wishing I could ride like that, and that I wanted to be cool, like those kids.

None of the black kids belonged to Cub Scouts or Boy Scouts. One summer I attended a two week camp at the Theodore Roosevelt Scout Camp on the Chesapeake Bay. There were scout troops from up and down the east coast. Turns out there were black scout troops. After camp craft courses, swimming classes, and so forth we all ate in the same large cafeteria together. I learned to swim in the Chesapeake Bay alongside black kids.

One evening, our scout leader and community organizer Mr. Powell stopped by our home to tell my Dad of a neighborhood plan to build a swimming pool. Each family would need to contribute $500.00 to make it happen. All four of us kids were seated on the couch anxiously waiting for our Dad to nod affirmatively to this plan. I mean a real swimming pool in our own community, no more wading in the nearby creeks. How could anyone say no?

One of the questions my Dad asked was "Would the families from the colored section be allowed in on this plan?"

"Ah, why no," replied Mr. Powell.

My Dad said "Well, I don't think we'd be interested."

By then I had learned that when my Dad spoke, that was the end of it. We just kind of sagged back on the couch. I never asked my Dad to explain his answer.

I recall at Halloween time the black kids were not allowed to come through the white neighborhood. They were permitted however, to come through the night before Halloween. Very few families had treats ready a day ahead. Nonetheless, the parents of the kids that came to our door I remember as being so quiet, humble, and happy for anything given to their children. Mom always had something ready.

Every year at Christmas time my Dad would take us kids over to the "colored section" and we would present a box of canned goods, dried fruits, and hard candy to Sarah and her children. Sarah was the lady who would come to our house once a week to help my mom clean. Sarah lived in a duplex with a noisy group in the second unit that seemed to change every year.

During July or August of each year the black chain gang from the county farm would come down our road swinging large hand-held scythes to cut weeds along the sides of the road for fire mitigation. They had a large wagon with hot steamy tar buckets and gravel to fill the potholes. They had a portable toilet on wheels with canvas sides. The convicts were off chain whenever they stopped.

The Virginia summers were always hot and humid. I used to make up a bucket of lemonade with ice cubes and paper Dixie cups. My Dad's only advice was "Son, just be sure to offer some first to the big guy on the horse with the shotgun." The men would swallow the lemonade in one gulp and then go back to work. Their hands were huge, dwarfing the Dixie cups.

My Dad grew up on a wheat farm in a large Mennonite family. My Mom, on farms from a Methodist family originally from Arkansas. My Dad let us kids pretty much learn about life on our own, just as he had done. So what did the returning WWII Navy veteran and his wife do with their four growing children who needed some sort of guidance beyond their experience? They joined a Unitarian Church. Without understanding I grew to like it. Once, later in life, I heard Garrison Keillor on National Public Radio's (NPR) *A Prairie Home Companion* say of the Unitarians "don't ever piss off a Unitarian, or they will come by and burn a question mark on your lawn."

In youth group we would sometimes attend the services of different church denominations. My favorite was the black church. The pastor was so fired up. They had an amazing choir and when they sang the hairs on the back of my neck would stand up.

In Sunday school we were often assigned to bring in a newspaper clipping and be prepared to discuss the contents. Having my paper route early on Sundays gave me the edge. One Sunday I brought in an article on the 1955 Montgomery, Alabama bus boycott highlighting the activities of Dr. Martin Luther King, Jr. There were schematic drawings of a bus indicating where whites sat and where black people had to sit, in the back. During the boycott, the black people were willing to walk miles to work, ultimately forcing the City of Montgomery to change their seating policy, allowing them to sit anywhere they chose.

Following grade school we moved to New York as my Dad changed jobs. We lived in Westchester County in a well-to-do community with a very competitive academic high school. It was an abrupt change from Virginia.

My essay on these experiences was evidently found acceptable. I was notified that I was to be a part of the 1962 Coe College summer service project.

Philip K. Ensley'65

I was a 19 year old freshman when I decided to participate in the 1962 Coe Summer Project in Tougaloo, Mississippi. I was working in the Coe cafeteria in January, 1962 when a good friend told me about the project and asked if I was interested in going. She was very persuasive, and then I talked to the college chaplain, Dr. John Walker, who explained the purpose of the project, which was to be two weeks of study and work in Jackson, Mississippi.

It was cold and snowy that January in Cedar Rapids, and the thought of going to a warm place like Mississippi was very enticing. The chance to learn about a different part of the United States while being able to work with the people there was just the experience I was looking for, so I said yes. I was from Chicago and knew little about the world outside of Chicago and Cedar Rapids.

The experiences I gained while at Tougaloo during June of 1962 never left me. I am so grateful for the opportunity that Coe provided to me during one of the most important and explosive eras in our country's history. We were at Coe during the civil rights movement, the buildup in Vietnam, and the assassination of President Kennedy. I would like to share my Tougaloo experiences with you as best I remember them, more than 50 years later.

William H. Schalk '65

As I revisit that period in my life at Coe when we were signing on to go to Mississippi, I've been unsure about what turned the tide for me. What was the exact purpose I sensed that caused me to decide to go on that trip?

I am African American and I come from a family who absolutely did not believe in going south of the Mason-Dixon line. Any relatives we had who lived down there would have to come north to visit us. Why go – a very strong family sentiment – where you aren't welcome, will be mistreated, or even killed?

We had the story of my maternal grandmother who had helped a friend escape the "misadventures" of a local sheriff and who then had to escape herself, leaving her family behind and fleeing north at the age of 14. She landed in Bakersfield, California and never saw her parents again. Years later she was reunited with some of her siblings who had come north to the eastern states. I thought we had good reason not to venture south.

So what was my motivation?

This was the period in my life when I had come to a strong faith in God's presence not only in this world but also personally within me. The salvation Jesus offers us through the cross had become real for me and I found that time spent seeking God through prayer, study, and daily devotions was a most treasured time of my day.

However, the racial climate was an overwhelming struggle for me as I encountered Christians who supposedly shared my "new birth" experience but were promoting separation among the races and segregated practices on Christian campuses. Thank goodness for other Christian students at Coe who encouraged me to keep my eyes on the Lord and not be swayed by those who misrepresented his message no matter how prominent their voices.

Also at this time, the civil rights movement under the leadership of Dr. Martin Luther King, Jr. was gaining momentum. The message that Dr. King articulated was a call to action imbedded in our deep Christian roots for a peaceful, non-violent, yet steady progression toward a goal that would meet the needs of our whole society. This was a unique message among those seeking justice and freedom – a message that spoke to white and black people alike.

Dr. King visited Coe the year before our Tougaloo trip, and his sharing was the beginning of a wake-up call for me to be a part of an effort to practice the teachings of Jesus by showing love and fighting ill-treatment wherever I encountered it.

The president of Tougaloo College, located just outside Jackson, Mississippi, came to Coe during a special convocation that spring. He shared the unique work that Tougaloo was doing using the talents, skills, and determination of a racially mixed group of students, teachers, and community activists. I listened with real interest to his compelling presentation. Tougaloo sounded like a "safe" place to witness firsthand the work of educating, promoting desegregation, and making a difference in that community, in the South, and perhaps in our whole nation.

Still, I was guardedly on board. I wanted to see behind the scenes of the events we saw on the news, to learn effective ways of bringing about change, and to learn how to live out my faith. This was it! I was hopeful.

Jean Johnson Sidner '63

Showing Up is Half the Battle

Figure 4: Arch and gate of Tougaloo Southern Christian College Welcoming Coe Students to Campus in June of 1962.

The Journey to Tougaloo

On Sunday, June 4, twelve students and Dr. Walker left the safe harbor of Cedar Rapids and headed south to Tougaloo in three cars. Our energy level was high, and we were also quietly apprehensive as we traveled to an area we didn't know much about.

Our destination was the Tougaloo Southern Christian College. The college is ten miles north of Jackson, the state capital. Tougaloo would be the base where we would live, study, and work as we learned about the issues and culture of that part of the South.

On the second day of travel, we tried to stop for lunch at two restaurants in Memphis, but were denied because one of our fellow Kohawks, Jean Johnson (Sidner), was an African-American. That didn't deter us, however, because we were able to stop for lunch later at a drive-in outside of Memphis. I remember having lunch on some benches by an outside table. We were repulsed by this experience, but were to learn in a few days that segregation was to be expected in the South.

On a personal level this experience stands out because two years later one of my teammates on the University of Chicago AAU Track Club told me about a similar experience. During the summer I would run on this AAU track team and compete against some of the best teams in the nation. One of my teammates was Willie May, who had won the silver medal in the 110 meter high hurdles at the 1960 Olympics in Rome. Willie told me that when he ran in the Mason-Dixon Games in Memphis he could not stay or eat in a "for whites only" hotel. The Mason-Dixon games were among the top track events in the nation, and even there, with some of the best athletes in the world competing, prejudice trumped goodwill and fairness.

William H. Schalk '65

We left Iowa on June 4 of 1962 in a Volkswagen, a station wagon, and another car. My memory of the drive down was listening to music, singing with the ukulele, and listening to Tom Palmberg tell the plot of *Black Like Me*, by John Howard Griffin, which he had recently read. It was published in 1961 and describes Griffin's six-week experience travelling on Greyhound buses (occasionally hitchhiking) throughout the racially segregated states of Louisiana, Mississippi, Alabama, and Georgia as a black man. I wondered what adventures would be ahead for us and what it would be like experiencing segregation.

I distinctly remember my reaction to the drinking fountains that we encountered at one of our rest stops as we entered Mississippi. I was at first confused that there were two and then shocked at the realization that those of us who were white had our own fountain, and that Jean Johnson was required to drink from the fountain for black people. That picture is still embedded in my mind like a snapshot in history.

Sally Fels Meyers '64

In 1962, at 19 years of age I had completed my freshman year, a biology major thinking about medical school. I was now traveling to Mississippi, a faraway land it seemed, where just two years earlier Freedom Riders were arrested en masse, many going to the State Penitentiary known as the Parchman Farm.

As we began our journey south on the morning of June 4, 1962. I remember a popular song of that time playing over and over on the car radio, Little Eva singing *Locomotion*. Ultimately, it reached number one on the charts.

There was no air conditioning in the cars then, and the air coming through the windows on our journey south was becoming hotter and heavier. What lay ahead weighed on my mind. I kept dated entries in my journal and will share some throughout this work.

June 4, 1962

That first night we stayed in a white clap-board tourist home just off the main highway in Kentucky. You could hear the heavy traffic not far away. After unloading the cars we sat around singing songs and enjoying each other's company. As I recall we even sang Kumbaya. Don't recall holding hands though, as the joke goes today.

Looking back we were just a bunch of college kids from Iowa. Little did we know what was about to come. We were all soon to be swept into events that would forever change our lives. In my journal was a note about the trip and the participants, "The cool air is sifting in through the porch door now and everybody is upstairs and almost asleep. I wonder what this trip would mean to each of them. Then, too, I wonder what it will mean to me as I mature. I wonder again as to how or if our trip will affect the kids at Tougaloo. I hope like anything that trouble will not befall our group."

> ### June 5, 1962
>
> *In Memphis for lunch we were refused at two restaurants, the second restaurant being a Howard Johnsons, because we were an integrated group with Jean Johnson. We began to see more and more "whites only" signs. We finally found a road side hamburger stand that would serve Jean but, even so, she had to go around to the back door to get her food.*

We were expected to arrive at Tougaloo that evening.
Philip K. Ensley '65

Starting the drive down to Mississippi, it soon became apparent this was not going to be your typical "off for two weeks of summer camp" kind of experience. While driving into the South, things that happened, conversations, observations, people met - all had quite an impact at the time, an intense eye-opening educational experience.

Experiences remembered, at least as I recall them now:

The first incident – our group stopped in Memphis for a hamburger, and were told that a fellow student, Jean Johnson, had to order from a window around back. Some of us thought "we'll just order from the same window she did." It was not readily accepted by the white staff inside. It quickly became apparent that "Dorothy, we're not in Kansas anymore!"

In contrast, we received a warm welcome and acceptance from the Tougaloo students when we arrived on campus and were given rooms in their dorms. We had easy conversations with them in their dorm rooms and over meals. They were interested in us and open in answering many of our questions.

We met various people, not all of us at every meeting/discussion, but we shared the conversations and our experiences: James Meredith, Medgar Evers, Governor Ross Barnett, Jackson Police, White Citizens Council members, local white and black pastors, YMCA/YWCA children, bible school staff and students, NAACP staff members, black church groups, local sheriffs, jailers, probable Ku Klux Klan members, black families, and more. What an intense exposure and educational experience!
Dale Ely '63

I had never been abroad – I don't think going to Canada counts – but going to Mississippi has to. We were in a foreign country.

The farther south we went, the more pronounced it became that we were no longer in Iowa, nor even in the United States as we had known it. This was clear not only from food choices (i.e., hamburgers didn't come with the usual condiments and forget decaffeinated coffee or ice tea without sugar) but from the fact that I was not welcome in all restaurants.

We were first turned away from a Howard Johnson's because of my presence. My maiden name was Johnson and for all I know, Howard may have been a distant relative, but that possibility didn't get us in the door. The color of my skin was a deterrent. On more than one occasion fellow students had to order something for me and bring it back as I waited in the car.

Being black in Iowa was not a discrimination-free experience, but I never had to endure the deep hatred of being so belittled that I was treated as invisible – an experience that occurred later in our journey when we were on a side trip. People would accost us as we got out of the car, throwing slurs at the other students without even looking my way. It was truly as though I wasn't even there. How profoundly demeaning.

Jean Johnson Sidner '63

Arrival at the Tougaloo Campus

In early June, 1962 I had just graduated from Coe with a history major and minors in English and secondary education. The day after graduation a group of Coe students, led by our chaplain Dr. John Walker, were to drive to Tougaloo College in Jackson, Mississippi to learn about the situation there and help in any way we could. Some of us stayed overnight at Judy Lamparek's home. We left early the next day in two cars and arrived safely at Tougaloo.

We stayed in dorm rooms and ate in the college cafeteria. This was the first time I had encountered sweetened iced tea and I asked if they had any unsweetened tea. They didn't and looked at me as if I were crazy to ask.

Vicki Burroughs Bixler '62

Figure 5: The Tougaloo College Church bell tower in 1962.

We arrived about 6 p.m. on the second day of travel. I was struck by the quiet beauty. Lush green grass and beautiful trees outlined the campus. The exterior of many of the buildings was wood because they did not have to go through the winter weather we experienced in Iowa.

The men's dormitory was an old wooden structure that reminded me of a World War II barracks. The beds were comfortable, but the air was more humid than I had ever experienced, which made it difficult to sleep. I don't believe the term air-conditioning was in anyone's vocabulary yet.

The students on campus were great – friendly, fun, and easy to get along with. We had many discussions with them in the ensuing two weeks about race, education, and the problems they faced.

The school cafeteria was quite an experience. We were introduced to grits, which most of us had never had before. The taste is hard to describe, but it is a staple in the South. Some of us got used to this "delicacy" and even looked forward to it at breakfast every day. To this day when I order grits, I think of Tougaloo.

The cafeteria staff gave us bag lunches when we went to Jackson for our work experience. I have never gotten over the chicken sandwiches they provided, which consisted of a full chicken breast (with bone) between two pieces of white bread. It took a long time to work through the carving process, but the meal was good and kept us going.

We knew before we arrived that Tougaloo was a predominately black college. What we didn't know was that it practiced integration in reverse - the faculty was half black and half white. One of the white professors we met was Dr. Ernst Borinski (hereinafter Dr. B), who was to be our primary contact while at Tougaloo. Dr. B was a social science professor from Europe, with a wonderful German accent, who served us dinner in his lab and then presided over an informal discussion and gave a little background on the college and the community of Jackson.

His lab before, during, and after we left Tougaloo was a melting pot for civil rights discussion, planning, and implementation. One evening Medgar Evers, Field Director of the NAACP in Jackson, attended one of our meetings.

I am purposely leaving out any further remarks, except for one, about Dr. B because I know others will also be writing about this great man. My one comment is that in the 54 years since our journey to Tougaloo, I never met anyone like him again. He understood the issues involved in race and civil right issues, and he knew how to make and implement change. Very few Americans have ever heard of him because he was behind the scenes as this cause moved forward in the '60s. He was the unselfish teacher who taught others how to lead and move the civil rights issue forward. He was a man for all seasons who is part of our rich history of social change in America.

William H. Schalk '65

Figure 6: Girls' dormitory on Tougaloo campus, 1962.

We finally arrived at Tougaloo. There were about 500 regular students, with a campus larger than Coe's, Spanish moss on all the trees. There was no formal reception for us. This, I would come to understand, was because many northern white groups had visited before us and so seeing us arrive was not an uncommon sight. I learned that, of Tougaloo's last graduating class of '64, 16 went on to graduate school outside of Mississippi.

Dr. Borinski, a man of Polish descent on the Tougaloo faculty, provided an orientation talk. He described the black person's position and that of the white community. We were to be given a great deal of freedom to visit classes, interview state legislators and NAACP leaders, talk to sharecroppers, townspeople, law officers, and the Citizens Council. While we were briefed on the voting laws and social laws of the state, Dr. Borinski desired that we not be biased in any way. To him everybody is an individual and should be judged accordingly. He indicated his sociology lab was the only place in Mississippi where white and black people could talk freely without being arrested. For black people and southern white liberals, Tougaloo was a sanctuary.

June 6, 1962

I visited a biology lecture in the new (1959) science hall. I was greatly impressed by this lecture because of the enthusiasm put into it by the black lecturer Dr. Andrews. Their facilities for physics, physiology, zoology, botany, and chemistry are quite good. Their labs are new and therefore outclass Coe's labs by far.

We visited their chapel, library, gym, dorms, new student union, and administrative buildings. I met Mr. Stevens who has been here for four years. He retired from teaching at Syracuse University several years ago. I met Ms. Trumpauer, a white junior who stands five feet and is a fireball when it comes to integration. She has led sit-ins and freedom rides, and is close to Dr. Martin Luther King. She has been in jail many times for as long as ninety days. I met her when she was talking to Mr. Stevens. They were discussing a black boy who was just put in jail for forgetting to carry his driving license with him. They acted very natural about the whole thing, as if it happened every day. They mentioned that the boy did not want to be bailed out, but Mr. Stevens casually said if they needed bail money he would be glad to pay it.

There are laws in the state that prohibit black people from being served at white eating places. Likewise laws prohibiting white people from eating at black eating places. The owner who violates these laws could have his license revoked. Guess who controls the license board, you guessed it, the (White) Citizens Council. Black peo-

ple pay taxes to build football stadiums yet they cannot enter the stadiums. One white student here got his face kicked in for talking to a black girl who was selling newspapers on the streets of Jackson.

Tonight we listened and participated in a panel discussion given at the sociology lab. Dr. Walker gave a speech concerning why we were in Mississippi. Then Dr. Borinski directed questions to us and we questioned him.

I am always embarrassed to talk in front of a large group, so after the meeting broke up I fired questions at him for over an hour. We talked until 11:30 PM and I'm writing at 1:00 AM in the morning. Dr. Borinski stated that it is not only the southern black people he wants to help, but more attention is needed to help the misinformed white population. To him the solution is seen as educating the South so they will become disgusted with the current culture and demand revision.

I feel like my patience is already at an end and I am fed up with a problem that has corrupted mankind so terribly that a horrible fear is present in my mind. It comes close to a nightmare. I want to help so bad.

There is an underground youth organization, yet you don't hear much about it. I don't know what the outcome of this trip will bring but by the time you receive these words I will probably be on my way to Minnesota. I hope you have had no fear for my safety, but it's already to the point where my life doesn't mean much unless I can help my fellow man. I can only follow my heart and what I have learned about human love, charity, and decency.

There is a 'hate' campaign going on in Mississippi. Children, parents, uncles are told to spy on parents, children, neighbors and report any liberal views. This has turned neighbor against neighbor and twisted the minds of the people of Mississippi. You cannot believe it until you see it. A man cannot speak freely in Mississippi. I am so ashamed of my fellow Americans. It is not the black people that need help, it is the white population.

Last night I cried.

Philip K. Ensley '65

We were told by Dr. B during one of our early meetings, that our group would probably turn out to be one of four types:

1. Making friends on campus
2. Interviewing people in Jackson
3. Volunteer work
4. Applying pressure for change

I am happy to say that we were all of these!
William H. Schalk '65

Observing Racism and Inequality

I remember many things about the Coe Summer Service Project in Mississippi, but my most vivid memories are these.

The shock of discovering that segregation was alive and well - in the "Land of Lincoln!" When we tried to have a meal at the Howard Johnson's in Cairo, Illinois, we were turned away. Wasn't this the North? Isn't HoJo's a national chain?

The feeling of unreality and anger when we first encountered the "WHITES ONLY" signs in the south. Although we knew about this, actually experiencing it was something else altogether.

The heat. And the Spanish moss hanging from the trees. The feeling of peace and safety on the green and shady campus.

Swimming at the Natchez Trace with a few white and black friends - and the white people already there getting out of the water.

A meeting in a country church on a very hot evening– nearly everyone using the paperboard fans placed next to the hymn books in the pews that advertised the services of a local funeral home.

A visit to rural tenant farm families: dirt roads, worn out wooden houses, bare feet, hard-packed yards, and friendly people.

The tension I felt in the simple act of walking on a downtown street in Jackson and going into the Woolworth's 5 and 10 – remembering Emmett Till and wondering, how does a black man avoid looking at a white woman on a crowded sidewalk or in a busy store?

Most of all, I remember our host and teacher, Dr. Borinski – affectionately called "Dr. B" by one and all.

Dr. B's lab and the campus dormitories provided an opportunity for us – mostly white – northerners to interact with southern – mostly black – students. Sometimes the interaction was a challenge to answer *why* we would want to come south, and especially, why come south when there is racism and related problems in the North? The students also wanted to know what we would *do* as a result of our visit.

At the time, I could only answer with "I'm concerned, and I want to learn." When I think about it now, I suppose I must be one of those life-long students: always curious, wanting to know, to look things up, to ask. I am especially focused on issues of individual human rights and social justice.

Dorothy McCarter Quiggin '62

Figure 7: Tom Palmberg (left) and Phil Ensley (right) in downtown Jackson, Mississippi, 1962.

Separate, Not Equal

Part of our responsibility on this trip was to do volunteer work. We each had a different function: working in a Methodist Community Center, YMCA, YWCA, Boy's Reformatory, or a vacation bible school in rural areas near Jackson and Tougaloo.

I volunteered in a black YMCA in Jackson. Fortunately, I had taken a course in games and minor sports at Coe the previous semester, so I was well prepared for the job. I worked during the morning hours and taught young students (4th - 6th grade) the fundamentals of different games and sportsmanship. I worked with a middle-aged black pastor who was a terrific role model for these kids. He had a wonderful Christian spirit that conveyed warmth and goodwill to the students.

The volunteer work gave us a chance to get into the community and meet and interview people, learn about the area, and also contribute to its well-being.

William H. Schalk '65

One thing not documented in my journal but well remembered was that when Bill Schalk and I first walked into the YMCA I noted how impressed I was with the facilities. There were beautifully tiled walls, glass, stainless steel, and an incredibly beautiful modern indoor swimming pool.

When we approached the office to report in as the students from Tougaloo, we were given an odd look and were told they knew nothing of any arrangements for us to be volunteering there. After an embarrassing pause we were told that we were at the wrong YMCA. Evidently the YMCA for black people was at another location, curiously enough on Lynch Street.

The facilities there were in stark contrast to the white YMCA. There was no indoor pool. The basketball court was a half court not a full court floor. The wrestling mats were in poor condition. There were no lockers or showers in the restroom.

Wednesday evening the men and women of our project discussed doing work at the "colored" YMCA & YWCA. The Day Camp at the YMCA which the boys will work at is located in Jackson. The boys are quite nice and very easy to talk to. I teach wrestling from 8 a. m. to noon and 2 – 5 p. m. We will start working next Monday. Mr. Fraser, the director of the YMCA, talked with us about race relations which we are starting to become an authority on. The main thing that has impressed me most is the fact that the black person has a sense of humor which has kept him sane.

June 13, 1962 - Yesterday we took five YMCA boys to the outdoor pool for black people in Jackson. It was the first time a white person had swam in that pool for three years. Bill Schalk and I got student games underway in the form of tag, etc. In less than 50 minutes the telephone calls rolled in asking if the pool were integrated.

Today, the YMCA director would let us go to the pool area but we could not swim in the pool. The pool itself is located in Jackson and is the only pool for black people. The director of the pool got his orders to keep us out of the water, although he himself didn't mind. He was too scared to tell us who had ordered the pool not to integrate.

Tomorrow we are planning to take five YMCA day campers to a Federal Park which is not liable to segregation.

Philip K. Ensley '65

We had a number of opportunities to work on campus and out in the Jackson community. I got to work in a "Y" that had services for children and youth. I remember feeling that I needed to quit school and just return to work there to address the basic rules of organization to run a classroom, how to organize and maintain supplies and materials, basic cleanliness and health care, and how to teach parenting or prepare healthy menus – the list went on and on. I felt there was so much I could offer right away that was needed. It just seemed unnecessary to finish my four-year degree when I already had such a great educational advantage.

Jean Johnson Sidner '63

Under-funded Public Schools

During my visit to a black high school near Jackson I found that Mississippi high schools were separate, but not equal.

There were a litany of problems: the faculty was understaffed, teachers were not well trained, salaries were poor ($2,400/year), laboratory equipment was non-functional or non-existent.

The typewriter classroom was especially bizarre because there were no typewriters on the desks. Instead, a photo of the keyboard was on each desk and students were expected to learn the keyboard by memorizing and touching the "keys" in the photo. Try that sometime and you will find how hard it is!

Before we left Cedar Rapids we were told that Mississippi ranked last in funding for schools in the United States. We were also told that the white schools had typewriters for their students. This issue was important for me because I was thinking about going into teaching at the time.

Apparently, Mississippi was still following the law established by the landmark 19th Century case *Plessy v. Ferguson* , 163 U.S. 537 (1896), where the Supreme Court's view was that "separate but equal" did not violate the equal protection clause of the U.S Constitution. This case was fortunately overturned in 1954 by *Brown v. Board of Education,* 347 U.S. 483 (1954) where the Supreme Court held that "separate educational facilities are inherently unequal."

Clearly, Mississippi was not following the law of the land and felt they could operate unchecked.

Where does Mississippi stand today on education? It seems that not much has changed. Last December, Jeff May, reporter for the Associated Press, used the town and public school of Durant, Mississippi as a reference and pointed out the school does not have any up-to-date textbooks and teachers must spend their nights on the Internet, searching for math and other problems to give their students. Since 2008, legislators have ignored a state law and spent $1.5 billion less on education than what's required. According to early estimates, the state could fall $280 million short again in 2016. Durant has 588 students in grades K-12. Teachers turn over quickly, according to the Superintendent, and when the district hires replacements, it tends to choose rookies expressly because they are cheap. (Source: *Racine Journal Times, Dec. 15, 2014, p. 10A.*)

Granted, many states in America today face similar problems, but Mississippi has not been able to change and improve their schools.

William H. Schalk '65

Interviewing Mississippi Governor Ross Barnett

I was fortunate to have a private interview with the governor in his office. I was very nervous going into the meeting because I had never met such a high ranking official before. I was also aware that he was a Sunday school teacher and also the leader of one the most biased states in the nation. When I went into his office I saw nothing but white throughout. The walls were white, the rug was white, and Gov. Barnett's suit was white. I realized that men often wear white suits in the summer because the area is so hot and humid, but all that white in one place was too much for me.

One of my questions to the governor was how he felt about black people in his state. He didn't say anything positive about them except that "many are fine athletes." Of course, none played for Ole Miss, but that was going to change in the years that followed.

In my mind, I couldn't understand how he could teach the Word of God on Sundays and be such a segregationist during the week. I didn't find the answer to that question until after I left, and it is quite simple: he was part of a culture that disliked or hated black people and did not want them to succeed socially or economically. He did not truly speak the words of Christ in Sunday School nor did he follow the words in the U.S. Constitution.

On September 29, 1962, Gov. Barnett was cheered by a capacity crowd of 43,000 at the Mississippi-Kentucky football game in Jackson, Mississippi, for refusing to allow James Meredith to enroll in the all-white University of Mississippi. The next day the Oxford campus erupted into riots against Meredith that had to be quelled by 3,000 federal troops. (Source: *New York Times*, November 23, 2014, Sports, p.4.)

James Meredith did get into Ole Miss in 1962, but it took President Johnson and people like Constance Baker Motley to make it happen. In a small way the twelve Kohawks on that historic trip to Tougaloo were able to witness and be part of the changing South.

William H. Schalk '65

Getting to Know the Tougaloo Students

My most rewarding and enlightening experiences were getting to know the people on the campus. Conversations about a recent sit-in at the Jackson Library revealed that our new friends had been bitten by police dogs and attacked by police officers. Black students were not allowed to swim in the municipal pool. Stools and chairs had been removed in most luncheon counters to make sure black people would not sit down.

Some of us taught Bible School at a nearby church in Jackson, others corrected test papers on campus. One day several of the girls grabbed rakes and manicured the lawn. This was an opportunity to talk to students as they passed to their classes. Many of the Tougaloo students seemed shocked to see us working and smiled as they walked by.

One day, Jean and I were in downtown Jackson and went to Woolworth's Dime Store to pick up some needed items. We hadn't had lunch, so we sat down at the front lunch counter. After waiting for some time, we decided to go to the counter for black people, located in the back of the store. We weren't too quick to realize that it wouldn't have taken much for some white people, irate just seeing us together, to cause a fuss and get violent, and for us to be thrown into jail. Even our friendship was illegal.

I had another eye-opening experience when Bettye Andrews asked me to walk with her and a couple of her friends to a sandwich grill right outside of the Tougaloo campus gate. We entered the grill and I heard the silence as soon as I walked inside. My blonde hair screamed "different" in the darkened room and I experienced another one of those snapshot moments in history. Everyone was staring at me. I didn't feel any anger or hate. I just felt the curiosity and amazement of the customers in the restaurant. I sat down with my friends and ordered a Coke from the waitress who wouldn't return my smile. I didn't feel fear or anxiety, just an awkwardness that I remember to this day and a love for the girls who included me in their group.

Sally Fels Meyers '64

Figure 8: Sprucing Up the Tougaloo Campus. Front row (left to right): Joan Johnson (Sidner), Carol Hackenhole (Straka); back row (left to right): Sally Fels (Meyers), Virginia Knight (Gute), Judith Laparek (Lanum).

Segregation at the Airport

One evening Bill Higgs and I went to the Jackson Municipal Airport for dinner. Bill was a 26 year old white attorney, a native Mississippian, and the legal advisor for the Jackson branch of the National Association for the Advancement of Colored People (NAACP). The purpose of the dinner was to show me how segregated the local airport was by using one area of the dining area as a ruse for white only dining and the other side for black people.

When we walked into the restaurant there was a private dining area designated for "airport employees only." The other side of the restaurant had counter service with only vertical posts and no seats. The waitress approached us after we entered and said "You can sit in the private area. The other area is for blacks." Bill and I had dinner and then departed.

The story would end here except we were setting up a trap for the airport personnel. As Bill and I walked out of the restaurant two of our colleagues walked in – one black and one white. They asked if they could sit in the private area and the waitress said "No, you have to be served at the counter". Clearly, there were two standards here: one for an all-white group and the other for black people, even if they were with someone white. We filed a complaint in Federal Court in Jackson the following day based on an illegal civil rights action.

Eventually, the municipal airport was re-named to honor Medgar Evers. It is now Jackson-Medgar Wiley Evers International.

William H. Schalk '65

The White Citizens Council

Tom Palmberg, Phil Ensley, and I pretended to be gung-ho segregationists and attended a meeting of the White Citizens Council. We were given propaganda pamphlets and hounded with pep talks encouraging us to start segregationist meetings and clubs back home. As you can tell from my earlier comments we were not impressed with their ideas or methodology.
William H. Schalk '65

June 9, 1962

This morning two guys and myself visited the lovely city of Jackson. We took pictures of some of the signs at the railroad station and at the stores. Some of the fountains are for colored people and the whites have their own fountain. We went through the court house and sat in the colored people section in the court room. The court room was not in session or else we would have been removed or arrested. We talked with the black folks and when we told them that we were from Tougaloo we became friends quickly. Then we asked around the courthouse to find out where the Citizens Council was located.

We entered the Citizens Council office and pretended that we were staunch segregationists and hated 'niggers.' They sucked this right in and deliberated greatly on segregation. I told Mr. Hallis, who is the head of the Council of Jackson, that we had terrible 'nigger' problems in Virginia, and he assured me that Senator Byrd was doing all that was possible to help our cause. He gave me tips on how to start a citizen's council in Arlington, Virginia.

Philip K. Ensley '65

Visit to Rural Areas Near Tougaloo

Some of us spent part of a day distributing clothes and food to cotton pickers in the rural areas. They were shy, yet pleased about having their pictures taken. We quickly realized that the environment of simple shack homes and run-down school buildings was a sharp contrast to schools in Jackson. Later we learned that one school taught black students typing by using paper keyboards.
Sally Fels Meyers '64

One of the most memorable visits for me was a trip to the rural area near Tougaloo. There, we saw black men and women working in the fields with a hoe, working the dirt and cutting the weeds. The rows were beautifully maintained, but the people were working for only $3/day. The homes where they lived were often broken down, with tin roofs that were red from rust and dirt. We saw one home with a man sitting on the porch with his three children.

The man told us that he was unable to work, so he took care of the house and children while his wife went to work in the fields. That scene was really hard to witness. Today, it is still burned in my memory as a symbol of the extreme poverty in Mississippi.
William H. Schalk '65

Figure 9: An unemployed share cropper tending to his children while his wife worked in the cotton fields, 1962.

I was not expecting to find people such as the Johnsons - a white family who lived as missionaries in the black section of Jackson. The family consisted of father and mother and three children. I stared at these blond-haired children who were called names on a daily basis that were usually reserved for black children. They endured this because they felt God had called them to serve the black community with household goods, tutoring, ministering through worship and bible study, and through a food shelf.

I could not imagine the personal sacrifice this family was making on behalf of God's kingdom and I worried for their children. I worried about the damage to their self-esteem and if they would be able to maintain a belief and trust in God. What an incredible witness they were to me, who had been struggling with people who looked like them and called themselves Christian, but couldn't welcome the likes of anyone who looked different from them. I would never forget the Johnsons.

Jean Johnson Sidner '63

June 9, 1962

Today at noon I met a (white) Rev. Johnson from Jackson who is helping the black peoples' cause greatly. He took me and one of the girls to see the black sharecropper's area out in the country. They're in poor condition. They don't have much protection, and Rev. Johnson has come within minutes of being mobbed by angry, stirred-up white people.

Philip K. Ensley '65

Figure 10: Rural life in the cotton fields on a hot and humid day, 1962.

Cultural Laws of Racism

It is against the law to advocate integration in any form. Right now there are no white students in Mississippi who can speak their mind and stay in good health. To tell the truth, there is no freedom of speech in Mississippi except at Tougaloo.

There are two kinds of law in Mississippi – cultural law (customs) and written law. If either is broken the punishment is the same. The courts of law are a farce. The judges are picked ahead of time and properly advised.

I asked Dr. Borinski if the Federal government has helped. He responded that the Federal judges have never lost a case. So the people of the Citizens Council keep the cases away from the Federal Courts. The Federal Court does not in any way affect the decisions of the state court.

Dr. Borinski is personally getting me interviews with some of the lawyers who have defended black people in civil and criminal law. I am also going to contact a few people who have served on juries.

Last night I talked with a black student here at Rust College. After asking him how he could stay sane under these Mississippi traditions, I questioned him as to why many black people were not socialist or communistic. He replied, "I think democracy is a great thing, and I'd like to see it work."

Philip K. Ensley '65

CHAPTER 4

Meeting Civil Rights Leaders

Medgar Evers

One of my favorite memories of Tougaloo is meeting Medgar Evers at one of Dr. Borinski's dinner parties at the lab. I did not realize Mr. Evers' significance and the role he played in the civil rights movement until after he was slain.

I remember Mr. Evers as being soft spoken, athletic, articulate, well groomed, and politically savvy. We spent most of the evening talking about athletics, football in particular. He played football in college, and I played football at Coe. I felt a great camaraderie between us.

Years later, I remember, when I worked in the Pentagon, how we would get to work on Monday and discuss the previous day's Washington Redskins game. The rest of the week would be devoted to nuclear war plans. It was a nice way to start the week. That's how it felt after meeting Mr. Evers.
William H. Schalk '65

Having an opportunity to rub shoulders with SNCC (Student Nonviolent Coordinating Committee) and CORE (Congress of Racial Equality) members brought us right to the center of the sit-ins and marches we had only seen on TV. We witnessed the passion and the articulate discourse in sharing trainings and plans for the dismantling of the racist institutions and practices that were inherent in Southern culture (and in the more subtle structures that characterized the North). At times this felt like another call to leave my studies behind and get involved where the real action was occurring.

I felt that Medgar Evers, the civil rights activist who became well known as an organizer for demonstrations, boycotts, and voter registration, presented a gentle, humble, hardworking response to the situations that were coming to the fore as black people refused to keep silent about injustices. He was older than the usual youthful activists we met in SNCC and CORE. He was a family man whose activities were less flamboyant and exciting. He worked through organizations taking a step-by-step approach as events presented themselves. I felt like I knew him and was interested in following his progress.

How painful it was that one year later, he was gunned down in his driveway as his wife and children heard and watched from inside their home.

Jean Johnson Sidner '63

James Meredith and Constance Baker Motley

James Meredith was the first black person to be admitted to the University of Mississippi, and Constance Motley was one of the attorneys who represented him in this historic event.

I met both Mr. Meredith and Ms. Motley during a strategy and planning meeting at a private residence in Jackson. The meeting, designed to help get him admitted to the University, was only known to a few people in order to ensure that public officials were not aware it had occurred. I was privileged to be there.

As I remember, Mr. Meredith was for the most part quiet during the meeting. He was slight in build and seemed to be an introvert. The person I was most impressed with was Constance Motley. She was smart, outgoing, enthusiastic, and articulate in working out strategies. She had a presence about her that one could not forget.

Later in life, I wondered what happened to her. After finishing law school in the late '80s I checked the national register for lawyers and found that she had become a federal court of appeals judge in Baltimore, Maryland and the first black woman to be appointed to a federal judgeship.

William H. Schalk '65

An equally outstanding experience for me was our small group visit with James Meredith, the young black man who integrated the University of Mississippi. To me, Mr. Meredith embodied a wholesome attitude and an objectivity that was refreshing and a particularly needed perspective for my learning at the time. He had an understanding of himself and others, as well as the dynamics of the use of power and privilege over others.

He shared that a trait we all have in common is the desire to see our own people thrive and survive. He felt that if the tables were turned and black people were the dominant race, the ones in control, the ones setting the rules and standards, we would behave just the way white people were behaving toward us. He believed it was time for a change and he had chosen this one thing to do – take the needed steps to integrate Ole Miss.

There was something so freeing and reasonable about that goal as he presented it. It lacked the emotional load I had been intent on putting on every circumstance and event. Life was what it was, and when you have an opportunity to do something about it, do it. He wasn't putting white people down but recognizing our common humanity and the need for change. This attitude was so helpful to me. It caused me to experience a new confidence and sense of freedom, and added to the feeling that life could be manageable and under control.

Jean Johnson Sidner '63

Dr. Ernst Borinski

Ernst Borinski (1901-1983), a white, Polish/German Jew, was a social science professor who came to the U.S. in 1938 to escape oppression in Nazi Germany.

At Tougaloo College, he used his status as an experienced outsider to investigate and expose the extreme racism and practice of segregation in Mississippi, and provided the safe space and open atmosphere for discussion, learning, and change to take place.

He invited white community members to the mostly black campus to interact with students in his lab in the basement of Beard Hall. There, he offered food and food for thought in the form of forums, seminars, and interviews with local clergy, businessmen, educators, activists, and community leaders. In fact, the lab eventually became the safe place for local activists to meet and plan strategy for "The Jackson Movement" in 1963, and "Freedom Summer," 1964.

What I learned from Dr. B, the students, and invited guests in his social sciences lab had a significant impact on me.

Dr. B led from behind. Students in his lab were in a learning environment in which real thinking happened. The experience helped students find their voices and become leaders in action for change.

I experienced the effectiveness of his teaching style, which was to provide opportunities for people to learn about current events from those with direct knowledge or personally involved in shaping them – then get out of the way. That experience, almost as much as the new information and concepts I learned, has stayed with me.

I remember only one piece of theory expressed in the lab, and to me it was a revolutionary thought: that education isn't the way to reverse racism. Rather, the key is changing and enforcing the law so that *behavior* changes; that attitudes change when behavior changes. And not just the behavior of the white population.

Dr. B urged the black students to *act* on the changes being enforced by the federal government. If the waiting room at the train station was no longer designated "Whites Only," black people needed to start using it – and the pool, and the public drinking fountains, and the washrooms at the Trace. Never mind that the benches had been removed from the station or the stools from the diner at the airport so whites wouldn't actually have to *sit* next to black people!

The most powerful learning experience in that lab was an evening spent observing a training session for students who would participate in a sit-in.

The theory of non-violent protest is a good one and it works. The reality of what must be endured while attempting to claim one's right to sit at a public lunch counter is something else altogether.

Reading or hearing about the vicious taunts and assaults that were common at the sit-ins is nothing compared to watching it happen – even in a simulation at a training session. It was an extremely disturbing and moving experience for me that resonated every time I read or heard about the many, many times non-violent action and brutal reaction continued throughout the '60s in the South.

I just don't know how the students found the courage and determination to participate in these actions. Their disciplined pacifism was nothing short of heroic.

Recently, when I went on the internet to look up Dr. B and Tougaloo College, I discovered that Memphis Norman, the student assistant in his lab, was the key participant in the historic 1963 sit-in at the Woolworth's lunch counter in Jackson. Memphis had resisted calls to action, and had even criticized fellow students who put their studies aside to protest segregation. However, his courage at Woolworth's that day made the headlines everywhere. The event kick-started "The Jackson Movement" and profound change in Mississippi.

Dorothy McCarter Quiggin '62

Figure 11: Dr. Ernst Borsinski (aka Dr. B), in 1962 – a humble man who influenced history.

One of my enduring memories of Tougaloo is of Dr. Ernst Borinski, professor of sociology, who hosted our group and facilitated many of our discussions and experiences. Unfortunately, I don't remember many of the names of my professors at Coe, but I do remember Dr. Borinski from that two week period. He made time for all of us, led good discussions, made the kind of comments or asked the questions that made you think deeply and question your own beliefs, motivated you to be open to the need for and possibilities of change. I didn't fully appreciate that experience with him until much later when I was in a position to work with and supervise people of different backgrounds and race.

This appreciation was further imprinted several years ago when I happened by chance to view a film on PBS, *From Swastika to Jim Crow*. It presented the story of a number of Jewish refugee scholars who escaped Nazi Germany in the 1930s and 1940s and found teaching positions at southern black colleges. Dr. Ernst Borinski and his teaching career at Tougaloo, 1947-1983, was a featured part of the film.

The film, derived from a book of the same title written by Gabrielle Simon Edgcomb in 1993, was produced around the year 2000. Unfortunately, I have not been able to view it again. Seeing this film peaked my interest to research it on the internet and then to search out links and further information about Tougaloo College. There I found information on the College's current fund drive to establish a "Dr. Ernst Borinski Endowed Chair."

Dale Ely '63

Attorney Bill Higgs

Bill Higgs became a good friend of mine and of Phil Ensley while we were in Tougaloo. In fact, he visited us several times at Coe in the ensuing years. Bill Higgs paid a heavy price for working with the NAACP and the civil rights cause in Mississippi, as his marriage fell apart due to the intense pressure on his family during the sixties. He was another unsung hero who deserves recognition for a job well done.

Mr. Higgs will play a prominent role in several of the stories that follow.

William H. Schalk '65

CHAPTER 5

Coe Students Harassed and Arrested

June 9, 1962

Also I met attorney Bill Higgs who was born in Mississippi, went to Harvard Law School, and returned to devote his life to justice in Mississippi. He asked me and two other guys if we would like to spend a weekend in the Delta regions of Mississippi where the South had its glory in the true plantation system. We are leaving Saturday morning and coming back Sunday evening.

Well as I mentioned in the last note, Dale, Tom, and I drove with Mr. Higgs to his home in the Delta which was 110 miles towards the Mississippi River in the town of Greenville. We had a shocking incident with the police of Belzoni City on the way. We were so shocked by our experience, that we wired a telegram to Attorney General Robert Kennedy. The telegram cost us $14.00 but, it was worth it. The following is a copy of the telegram:

Traveling through Mississippi today, at 10:00 o'clock A.M. we, a group of Iowa students, stopped to examine a Negro dwelling on the outskirts of Yazoo City.

We proceeded north-west and were stopped at 11:00 o'clock by the chief of police, Nichols, on the outside of Belzoni. He had been waiting for us at the request of the Yazoo City Police. He demanded that we explain why we had 'stopped to talk to those niggers.' He was armed with a pistol and accosted us in a threatening manner.

> The auto was searched. We were warned not to 'fool with the niggers' on the rest of our journey. After a frightening warning concerning the consequences of Mississippi tradition, we continued our trip shocked by the police-state tactics on United States Highway 49 West. As citizens of the United States, we demand immediate investigation and correction of this terrifying and unforgettable incident. We are currently visiting at Tougaloo Southern Christian College in Jackson, Miss."
>
> Phil Ensley, Scarsdale, N.Y.
>
> Dale Ely, Canton, Ill.
>
> Tom Palmberg, Burlington, Iowa

When the police officer in Belzoni stopped us he walked toward the rear of the vehicle and requested Tom open the trunk. He likely had never seen a VW Beetle or he would have known that all he'd see was an engine compartment. It was apparent he did not know the trunk was in the front of the vehicle. The officer then proceeded to walk around to the front of Tom's car to see inside the trunk all the while fondling his holstered revolver. While we thought this rather comical, our demeanor remained deadly serious. As soon as the sheriff departed, Bill Higgs told us to write down all that we could remember of the details of this encounter.

Sometime later I learned this same sheriff approached a black soldier in his uniform sitting on a bench waiting for a bus, and when the soldier did not move fast enough the sheriff pulled that pistol and killed the soldier.

Mr. Higgs is a close friend with the editor of the *Delta Democrat & Times* of Greenville, the most liberal newspaper in Mississippi. He introduced us to the editor, Hodding Carter, a Princeton graduate. Both he and his father have written many books concerning the South. He is quite interested in our story and phoned it in to his paper and also U.P.I. and the Associated Press.

Mr. Carter gave us a tour of the *Delta Democrat & Times* newspaper building where the press was located on First Street immediately behind the levee, where in the distance one could see the Mississippi River. The presses were "rolling" and the entire building seemed to shake. I learned that Hodding Carter's father by the same name, and editor before his son, had been awarded a Pulitzer Prize for his objective and progressive reporting of social issues in Mississippi, including his editorials concerning civil rights. Because of his reporting on civil rights, Hodding had received threats, and at night he had a very large man with a very large club standing watch.

That evening, Saturday, we picked up the Sunday edition of the *Delta Democrat* and sure enough it was on page one. Our fame not only reached the Jackson newspapers, but also an article appeared in a Memphis, Tennessee paper. On Sunday June 10, after seeing our names in three newspapers and hearing our report on radio news, we decided to take a different route home and not stop in Belzoni. We traveled to Jackson by way of Vicksburg and drove through the Federal park set aside as a battle monument similar to Manassas in Virginia.

June 9, 1962 - When we got back to Tougaloo, everybody had already heard about our encounter with the Belzoni police. Rev. Johnson asked us if we would testify before the Civil Rights Commission concerning this incident and sign an affidavit.

I forgot to mention that our incident at Belzoni has been ripped apart by the papers of Jackson in order to make the sheriff of Belzoni look justified. We are answering these falsifications in the form of the affidavit which I spoke of earlier which will be submitted to the Civil Rights Advisory Board next Wednesday.

Philip K. Ensley '65

What an opportunity was presenting itself! A young white lawyer engaged in helping and encouraging black politicians invited a small group of us to accompany him to a strategizing meeting. A black gentleman who had run for office was in the process of reviewing his effort, along with his supporters. William Higgs, the lawyer, had offered his support and legal services in such situations. He had connections in Washington to Robert Kennedy to help oversee his safety as he went about this political work.

I loved travel and was excited about this opportunity, especially since there was a chance that we could see Ole Miss and visit William Faulkner, the author/playwright. We did get to visit Ole Miss, but Mrs. Faulkner said her husband wasn't faring well and couldn't receive any visitors. In July of that year, Mr. Faulkner died.

Somewhere along the way to the meeting, William, the lawyer, noticed that we were being followed. As we left a county, a police car (sometimes unmarked) would be waiting for us and would begin following us.

When we entered Clarksdale, the car following us signaled us to pull over. We were summoned to follow him because we were "under suspicion." We were taken to the Clarksdale jail. Vicki and I were separated from the men in our group and William was taken away separately.

I was called to talk to the sheriff at some point. As I answered his questions with a "yes" or "no," he suddenly yelled at me.

"Can't you say 'yes, sir,' 'no, sir?'"

I yelled back at him, "NO!" This was a totally automatic response, a response that let me know I probably would never have made it as a freedom fighter or demonstrator.

I was immediately hustled out of there and taken up a long flight of stairs to where black people were kept. I learned later that the sheriff had told William that he was going to put me with the criminally insane and let them have their way with me. It was a mercy that I hadn't been told that, for I was already visualizing my obituary in my hometown newspaper, *The Des Moines Register*. I truly thought I would never get out of that jail alive.

I was put in a cell that had a cot with a bare mattress and a toilet. There were a couple of men in the cell next to me who had a jagged mirror that they could stick out of the bars of their cell in order to see me and talk to me. The only problem was I never knew when they were going to "check" on me – I didn't dare use the toilet.

My only other company was a nine-year-old boy who went by the name of Jesse James. Jesse said he was doing time for stealing a pack of cigarettes. He was free to roam around this upstairs area and visited me often.

I can't say my faith was strong, but I felt very clearly that I was in God's hands and I tried not to worry about how things would turn out. God would be present.

I don't remember having food to eat, so I assume that it was fairly early the next day when we were released. William's mother had tried to find us when she didn't hear from him, and I understand that Robert Kennedy's office was contacted and local people were called to trace where we had last been seen. Our car was discovered outside the jail and the sheriff had been called and ordered to release us.

I was taken separately from my fellow students to the home of a prominent black family in the area. We didn't want to continue traveling together, arousing the suspicions of local authorities. Later I was driven back to the Tougaloo campus.

Jean Johnson Sidner '63

Figure 12: Jail Cell in Clarksburg, Mississippi, where Coe students were held for one scary night.

June 18, 1962 - This journal note was written from the Coahoma County Jail on the back of the Oxford-University (University of Mississippi) campus map I had acquired earlier on our visit to the University of Mississippi, as I did not bring my journal on the trip to Clarksdale. This is sort of a supplement to my notes on this project. I earlier mentioned that on our trip to Ole Miss we would stop and watch the proceedings of a black campaign meeting for Rev. Lindsay who lost his congressional race. He is trying to get into Congress. After the meeting we were picked up by the Clarksdale police for a trumped up charge of investigation.

It is Monday, and therefore I'm writing this letter in jail. They are capable of holding us three days and nights. If they do, I won't be able to reach Minnesota on time.

They haven't let us make any phone calls yet. They split us up. They took Jean Johnson to one cell, Vickie Burroughs to another cell, Bill Higgs to one cell and Dave Campbell and I were put into another cell which already had four juvenile delinquents in it. Last night we could hear the guards take Bill Higgs for questioning. One of the trustees said he was able to get off a couple phone calls, so he probably called Dr. Walker. But the trustee didn't know for sure.

Guess what, I'm only about 36 miles from Helena, Arkansas, where my mother was born.

Dave Campbell, 19 years old, will be a junior at Oberlin College and is helping Bill Higgs this summer in his voter-registration project. He is also writing articles in the Mississippi Free Press.

The police down here are bad news. They won't tell you a thing or try to help you. It even makes you madder when you know you have done nothing to go to jail. There is something terribly wrong down here.

Our civil and constitutional rights had been violated something frightfully. It all happened so fast and the many details of the arrest became a blur until later. The report of our arrest and subsequent release was detailed in the Jackson, Mississippi papers and the *New York White Plains Reporter Dispatch* (page 13) and across the nation as well. At home the black mail man who had delivered mail to our home for countless years knocked on my parent's door and thanked them for what their son had done.

Philip K. Ensley '65

We also met Bill Higgs, a local white civil rights lawyer. He asked if some of us would like to accompany him to an NAACP meeting in Clarksdale, Mississippi. Phil Ensley, Jean Johnson, and I volunteered to go, along with Dave, an Oberlin College student.

Bill picked us up on a Sunday morning and drove us to Clarksdale where the meeting was held in an African American church. Part of the discussion at the meeting was how to pay off campaign expenses for a black candidate for Congress who had been defeated in the primary election. It was late afternoon when the meeting adjourned. The five of us got into Bill Higgs' car and drove out of town. We had the uncomfortable feeling that we were under surveillance.

As soon as we left the city limits, we were pulled over by a county sheriff's deputy. We were instructed to follow him to the county jail, where we were incarcerated without being allowed a phone call. When we asked why we were being held, they said we were "under suspicion."

The jail was of course segregated. Jean, my friend from Des Moines, was in a cell for African American females. She was a music major, so she said she did scales to keep from being afraid. The three men were in the white male section of the jail. I was locked up alone in a room with a bed and bathroom facilities that was apparently the white female area. There was one book, Kitty Foyle, which I had almost finished by the next afternoon. I was very apprehensive, but the only time the deputy came in was to bring meals. I remember a hot dog dinner.

We were held overnight, until 2 the next afternoon. By that time Bill Higgs' mother had called someone to find out why we had not arrived at her house to stay overnight, as planned. So the word got out that we were being held. Someone had called the Attorney General's office in Washington, and the news was on the radio. So the sheriff apparently decided to let us go. Before we were released, he called me into his office and interviewed me about why we were down here and warned us to go back north and mind our own business.

After we were released, we did go to Bill Higgs' parents' house in Greenwood, Mississippi to stay overnight. They had a snow cone stand in front of their house and his mother said they had put their two sons through college with the profits from that stand. Bill made some phone calls and we were to testify before a federal grand jury in Jackson, Mississippi the next day. We did testify about our treatment in Clarksdale. There is a picture of Jean and me coming down the steps of the courthouse that was on the front page of the Des Moines Register the day after.

Since we knew we would be in the news, we had to call our families and let them know we were alright. My whole family (parents, six younger brothers and sister, grandparents and aunt) had been at my graduation. My mom, Mary Pooley Burroughs '39, and aunt, Eleanor Pooley '36, were Coe graduates. But my parents were in Colorado, dropping my brother Paul off at the Air Force Academy for his first year there, so I didn't know where to call them. I had to call my grandparents in Greene, Iowa and have them relay the word.

Many years later, I found a box of newspaper clippings that my mother had saved about my misadventures in Mississippi, including an article Dr. John Walker had written, explaining our purposes in going south. We were really there to help and to see for ourselves what life in the segregated South was like. We did not intend to cause problems. The president of Tougaloo College had been a speaker at Coe the previous spring and had invited Dr. Walker to bring a group of Coe students to visit Tougaloo. For us this was a service project and a chance to see a part of the country we had not been to before.

1962 was an important year for me. I turned twenty-one, graduated from college, became engaged to Robert Bixler, moved to Chicago, found a job at the *Chicago Sun-Times* and was married December 22nd in Greene. Jean sang at my wedding. My husband and I moved into a small apartment on the north side of Chicago.

Early in the new year there was a knock on our door and an FBI agent was there with a subpoena requiring me to testify before a federal grand jury in Oxford, Mississippi. I said I couldn't afford to fly there and he said the government would pay my expenses. So I flew to Oxford by way of Memphis and discovered that Jean Johnson was also on the flight to Oxford. All of us were there to testify.

After we made our appearance, we were in a taxi on the way to the airport when Jean asked to stop at a drugstore to buy something she needed. So we stopped and she went into the store. This caused a problem and the police were called. We ended up at the police station. They weren't sure what to do with us, so one of the guys explained that we were on our way to the airport and wouldn't bother them again. With a sense of relief we were on our way.

Several years later, Bob and I and family drove to Mississippi to visit his sister and her family, who lived in Byhalia then. I was still uneasy about visiting the state. But we have been back many times since and had good experiences. We knew times had changed when we heard that Phil Ensley had visited Clarksdale and found that the sheriff was now African American.

Vicki Burroughs Bixler '62

Students Released in Jackson

THESE FOUR college students and attorney William L. Higgs, second from left, appeared before the Mississippi Civil Rights Advisory Committee yesterday in Jackson, Miss., to tell about 20-hour incommunicado arrest in Clarksdale, Miss., Saturday. They were in a racially integrated student group, released without charges after being jailed overnight. They had attended a Negro church meeting to discuss the Rev. Merrill Lindsey's unsuccessful campaign for Congress. Students, left to right, are Phillip Keith Ensley of Scarsdale, N. Y., and Coe College, Iowa; Jean Johnson, Des Moines, Iowa; David F. Campbell, Tulsa, Okla.; and Vicki Burroughs of Iowa. — AP Wirephoto.

Figure 13: Left to right - Phil Ensley, Attorney Bill Higgs, Jean Johnson (Sidner), David Campbell, and Vicki Burroughs(Bixler).

CHAPTER 6

Social Events

There were plenty of social events both on and off campus. Dr. Borinski's Wednesday night dinner parties stand out because of their social and intellectual character.

One evening we attended a party set up by Rev. Johnson, a white pastor who worked with black people in the area. He was not popular with white folks because of his ministry with black people, and for that reason, our evening picnic was held in the back of a pasture by a pond, away from others in the area. There were about fifty excited kids and twelve excited Kohawks and other guests at the picnic. There were songs, games, good food, and a lot of love shared that evening.

As I look back on our trip I believe there was a perfect balance between body, mind, and spirit. We got to walk, swim, sing, teach, and learn. We didn't forget that this was also a mission that encompassed the spirit of Coe and our Christian faith.

William H. Schalk '65

Figure 14: Enjoying a camp fire party with our new friends. Front row (left to right): Sally Fels (Meyers), Bill Schalk, Dot McCarter (Quiggin); back row (left to right): Virginia Knight (Gute) and Judith Lamparek (Lanum); other names unknown.

My most vivid memories are of several students who gravitated towards our group and our activities. Jimmy Armstrong had a ready smile and the ability to tease and entertain. Bettye Andrews was outgoing and eager to connect with us. We spent evenings in the girl's dorm, talking about hair texture and styling, families, and sit-ins that occurred in Jackson. We got to know a family that lived within walking distance of the campus and were invited to a picnic. We toasted marshmallows and sang around the campfire. We very much resembled a family reunion.

Sally Fels Meyers '64

June 16, 1962

Yesterday evening when we arrived at Rust College we went to a dance which turned into a great twist party. We all had a terrific amount of fun.

Philip K. Ensley '65

Figure 15: Taking a Break in Vicksburg, Mississippi. Bottom row (left to right): Rosalee Sutton (Olson), Chaplain John Walker: back row (left to right): Dale Ely, Vicksburg resident Mary Una Head, Carol Hackenholz (Straka), Virginia Knight (Gute), Dorothy McCarter (Quiggin), Bill Schalk; top row: Sally Fels (Meyers). Vicki Burroughs (Bixler), Jean Johnson (Sidner), and Philip K. Ensley were in Clarksdale at the time of this photo.

CHAPTER 7

Life After Tougaloo and Coe

The experiences I encountered during those two weeks on the Tougaloo Campus, right outside of Jackson, Mississippi were the most formative events in my life. Every important decision I have made since then reflects the awareness that grew within me that summer. The images stayed in my mind: whites only drinking fountains, the refusal to be served at Howard Johnson's, the stories that our new friends told us about not being allowed to use the city swimming pool, sitting with Jean at the Woolworth's counter, the dogs' tooth marks on the students who took part in a nonviolent sit-in at the Jackson Library. This just wasn't right!

What I experienced in Tougaloo influenced all the important decisions I made in my life. "Tougaloo" became my code word for decision making.

When I met with President McCabe in his office to decide my future after graduation—whether to go back to Amana to teach music or go into social work at McCormick Seminary in Chicago.

Tougaloo - Decision Made!

In 1966, when I said yes to Craig Meyers, a seminary student with a risk-taking approach to life, but a heart and mind that led to doing what was right.

Tougaloo - Decision Made!

In 1970, when we adopted David, born of a black father and white mother in Cincinnati, Ohio, even though both sets of our parents strongly opposed this decision. when the Indiana town we lived in still had a law not allowing a black person to stay overnight, and with our neighbor cleaning his gun on the front porch - the answer was:

Tougaloo - Decision Made!

We brought David home to a hostile environment, but before long our friends and church congregation soon grew to realize that David took breaths in and out just like a white boy. Strangers still expressed their concern and disfavor through frowns and mean looks when we were in public places. The County Case Worker had been very much against our decision to adopt a child of mixed heritage. After we got David, I made a concentrated effort to show him off to the child welfare office to try to change their minds. We left Remington about a year later after Craig received his doctorate and we discovered that faculty in the nearby town of Rensselear, a college community, were adopting children of mixed heritage.

In 1972, we adopted Danielle, a beautiful baby girl with a black mother and white father. Our new church home in Kokomo, Indiana was receptive to our mixed family. However, there were times when our children knew we were not the normal family. When Danielle was in nursery school at our church, I poked my head in the door of her classroom, and Danielle said "Hi Mom!" She came home that day and said that a friend of hers said that I couldn't be her mom, because I was white.

We served another church in Richmond, Indiana where our children experienced the "N" word. They came back from their swimming lesson early, crying and feeling very much alone and different. One such time, they were recounting bullying while I was driving them home. I stopped the car by the side of the road, trying to calm the anger that was rising within me and told them, "If anyone calls you that name, feel sorry for them. They have a problem, not you!" That has been our answer all these years.

In 1983, we moved to Texas. We found ourselves in a city rich with many different cultures. We had many opportunities to attend African American and Latino churches, where we were the only white people in the room. Through the years we have become family and the relationships have enriched our lives.

Tougaloo - Decision Made!

Craig and I became life members of the NAACP, Craig serving as Vice President, while I served on the yearly Freedom Banquet committee. We brought in Ruby Bridges, who integrated William Franke Elementary School in New Orleans in 1960, as a featured banquet speaker and presenter to city schools.

As Tom Green County Library's Children's Librarian, I was aware of the book, *Through My Eyes*, written by Ms. Bridges. Through the cooperation of the NAACP and our Public Library, we provided programs for San Angelo children and adults about a subject that was evident in our community: racism. The newspaper published letters the students wrote to Ms. Bridges about their feelings of racism in San Angelo.

In our 30 years in San Angelo, most of our lives and ministry have been spent working with colleagues in African American and Latino communities, developing a multi-cultural church and working in community organizing, breaking down racial barriers, and promoting fair housing. When a school was shut down in an African American neighborhood and the children were bused to another school, the Martin Luther King Celebration committee built a memorial with kids painting tiles with the theme, *I have a Dream.* The structure stands in Martin Luther King Park and is the pride of the community.

Tougaloo - Decision Made!

In 2012, the committee that both Craig and I serve on, The MLK Celebration committee held a Memorial Washington March on August 24. The following year we had the 50th Anniversary March with over 500 people marching to the San Angelo City Hall. I was part of the program to tell about Coe College's activities in Mississippi in 1962. I prefer to stay out of the limelight and promote diversity in a less public venue. However, after telling my story, I found that people embraced us for making right choices.

Every year, we have a four day celebration of Dr. King's birthday, including Youth Night, Gospel Fest, Community Worship Services and fellowship. Money collected during this time and other fundraisers provide college scholarships for students of color given upon their graduation from high school.

Tougaloo - Decision Made!

As a children's librarian, serving on Texas State book selection committees, I had the opportunity to speak up for multicultural literature so that all children of all races could see themselves in books. Many times, I met with all-white committees with no representation from the African American or Latino cultures, let alone Asian or Native American. I found myself as the only real advocate, having raised multi-cultural children, and having experienced Mississippi in the '60s. It was not that the people were bigots; they were just narrow in their experiences and hadn't lived the struggles.

When meeting with school groups, or individuals, I am always surprised that people are amazed at stories of the '60s. I am always astounded at the racism that still exists. We must keep the stories alive and make books available to our young people that tell it like it was. We are not at a loss for African American authors and illustrators. A short list of recommended reading appears at the end of this book.

Craig and I went back to Tougaloo in 2007. We visited Dr. Borinski's gravesite, the library archives, and the chapel where Dr. Walker preached and we sang "Steal Away to Jesus" with the Tougaloo Choir.

I have made many efforts to connect with some of the friends we made 54 years ago. In September of this year I called the Tougaloo Alumni Office and got several phone numbers which I called to try to locate Jimmy Armstrong and Bettye Andrews. I was unable to make connections with them. However, I spoke to some very interesting people who are graduates of Tougaloo. We had interesting conversations and they seemed pleased by my interest.

I received two letters in 1962, shortly after our visit. I have treasured them because they give the perspective our new found friends had of our three weeks in Tougaloo. I am still eager to reconnect with Bettye, Jimmy, and Alexander. Remembering their friendship 54 years ago I would like them to know their influence on my choices as I lived my life.

This is the path I have taken. I am grateful that Coe College had the faith in me to send me to Tougaloo in the summer of 1962 and for my breakthrough into the "outside world."

Today, I sit at my desk in the children's department of Tom Green County Library in San Angelo, Texas. A reminder is taped to my computer, where I serve the children and answer their questions.

It says, "Children may forget what you said...but never forget how you made them feel."

Tougaloo - Decision Made!

Sally Fels Meyers '64

I've been asked the question many times, "How did the Tougaloo experience change your life?"

I believe I have a greater appreciation for the inequities in our society and for the value of community service. I've also learned to judge a person by their character and not by the color of their skin.

After graduating from Coe in 1965 I went on to the Navy flight school in Pensacola, Florida. I served for twenty years, retiring with the rank of commander. During my Navy career, I met and served with thousands of people from many ethnic groups and always noted their ability to get the job done, not their race.

After retirement, I went to law school and became a district attorney. From this perspective I saw a real need for the education of our minority children. There were too many crimes being committed by minorities, and two of the key components for this were poverty and lack of education. I decided, after seeing this first hand, that I needed to be closer to the action of educating our youth. As a result, I served on our local school district's school board (the third largest in the state) for nine years, either as president or vice-president. The focus of my attention was to improve education for everyone, but especially the minority students who often had to overcome poverty and a one-parent household to succeed. As President of the Board, I was able to get our newest school named after a Racine civil rights leader from the '60s. That school proudly bears the name of Julian Thomas.

Fifty-three years after Tougaloo, the mission of erasing prejudice and establishing social and economic equality continues. The twelve Kohawks who went to Tougaloo had an amazing experience, and many have continued their life's journey by trying to rid the world of prejudice and establishing equality for all. Part of this drive was established at Coe.

William H. Schalk '65

In October 1962, Dr. King visited the Coe campus. I was asked to be on the student welcoming group and had the opportunity to have dinner in the Voorhees Hall cafeteria with Dr. King at a small table with a few other students. I remember leaning over and telling Dr. King about the Montgomery bus boycott newspaper clipping and proceeded to explain the boycott. He listened so carefully displaying a gentle smile.

Later I thought to myself I must have sounded pretty stupid explaining this historic event to the man who organized and led the boycott, a man ultimately considered to be the greatest orator and leader of social change in our time. Looking back he was so young. It was an experience as a sophomore student I shall never forget.

During my sophomore year at Coe I stayed in touch with Bill Higgs. I wanted to return to Mississippi to work on a voter registration project during the summer of 1963. My parents were concerned for my safety. They were right and, let's face it, they were paying my tuition at Coe. Thus we compromised and I worked that summer as a staffer for the Northern Student Movement (NSM) based out of Yale University. I was assigned to work in Washington, D.C. on a tutorial project designed to pair up summer government interns from colleges all over the country with grade school and high school students in the District who sought assistance in studying the texts they would be using in the fall at their respective schools.

I would often see Bill Higgs who was involved in several lobbying efforts. He introduced me to Roy Wilkins, then head of the NAACP, James Farmer of the Congress of Racial Equality, and I even sat in with Bill and soon to become Associate Justice on the Supreme Court, Thurgood Marshall, discussing upcoming voting rights legislation. Bill had become my mentor and good friend.

However the NSM staff gradually morphed into an activist group that wanted to go after a D.C. banking institution whose hiring practices were decidedly biased against hiring black people. The African Americans on our staff moved in a direction that the nationally based SNCC leadership was taking and that was to slowly reduce the influence of whites within civil right organizations. So I became discouraged and decided the politics of the civil rights movement was too much and resigned my position. I spent the balance of the summer working at a local car wash near our home in New York. I returned to my junior year at Coe soon to be consumed in studying organic chemistry.

During Christmas break 1963, I got a call from Bill Higgs to meet in New York City at a Students for Democratic Society (SDS) meeting. Bill called Bob Dylan from the coffee shop phone where we had met. In walked folk rock star, "Blowing in the Wind," already a music legend, Bob Dylan. We grabbed take out coffees and conversed while walking to the SDS meeting near Washington Square. The meeting rhetoric was confusing, argumentative over goals, unorganized, and I soon departed. Bill, seeing me leave, followed along presenting possible options for employment the next summer. I told him my thoughts of a career course change, and that the next summer I was going to find work at a veterinary hospital and consider a career in veterinary medicine. It was a difficult moment. I knew he would be disappointed by my decision. He went back to the meeting. I took the train back to Westchester. I never saw or heard from Bill again.

Philip K. Ensley '65

Following the Tougaloo summer, I returned to Coe for my last year. The next several years I was immersed in other endeavors; the Tougaloo experience kind of fell by the wayside.

I volunteered for the Peace Corps to serve two years in East Pakistan, now known as Bangladesh, constructing roads, bridges, and buildings. Following that, I was involved in State-side Peace Corps training programs, training new Volunteers going to India to work on construction and well-drilling programs. Then, I again volunteered for the Peace Corps and went into the Terai region of Nepal working on agricultural extension programs training villagers in methods of planting new strains of rice and use of fertilizers.

Both experiences, Tougaloo and Peace Corps, have made a significant impact on my life, coming from small town middle America. Unfortunately, my college career was less than stellar; however, I know that being a Coe student helped open the doors to Tougaloo and Peace Corps for me. Observing the poverty, lack of education, and the opportunities it provides, discrimination and abuse of civil rights during both experiences has shaped how I've lived my life, how I've worked and managed others, and how I've voted and continue to volunteer.

My thanks to Dr. John Walker, Dr. Ernst Borinski, fellow Tougaloo Project members, Peace Corps and fellow volunteers, villagers, and to those I met and who shared their lives and stories in each period of time.

Dale Ely '63

What have I done with the experience? My graduate studies were in social work, majoring in community and organizational development. In my 50 years as a social worker, I've had the opportunity to work in the women's movement, as a community organizer, as a program developer, and as a manager responsible for developing and leading anti-oppression work at a community health center.

My world is a bigger place than it was at age 21 in Tougaloo, Mississippi, and I think I'm a bigger person. I am grateful for that.

Dorothy McCarter Quiggin '62

June 16, 1962

Earlier I mentioned, in my notes, how mad I could sometimes be while listening to people condemn black people. Yet, now I see that we must understand these people. We must try not to hate them as people, but instead hate the ideas which have been drilled into their heads. Our greatest hope lays in educating the white community.

Philip K. Ensley '65

W hat were my final thoughts on going south? That trip was a gift to me. It deepened my understanding and acceptance of the complexities we encounter just by being inhabitants of this earth; and it deepened my faith that God is above all the circumstances and events that come into our lives, and that we are able to order our lives in ways that can make a difference.

This experience helped shape who I am. I had begun my studies considering a major in art and I found, after that trip, that sociology was more to my interest with a desire to study social work upon graduation. I found work in the non-profit sector working with underprivileged populations in areas such as literacy, parenting classes for court ordered individuals, programs for the homeless, and extensive work in a shelter for battered women and their children.

After taking time to raise our family of four, I later attended seminary and became an ordained United Methodist pastor, which has been the joy of my life. I am now retired and have had the pleasure of continuing to work part time as a United Church of Christ visitation pastor.

I credit the opportunity to have been a part of that Mississippi adventure with being the catalyst that helped reveal God's call on my life.

I am indebted to my fellow travelers, the students and staff who accompanied me, and to Coe College for this time of sharing our incredible journeys. This has given me a reason to look more deeply into that reservoir of experiences from the Tougaloo Summer Project of 1962.

Many thanks!

Jean Johnson Sidner '63

Recommended Reading

All ages

The Civil Rights Movement in America from 1865 to Present by Patricia and Fredrick McKissack
Freedom Walkers, The Story of the Montgomery Bus Boycott by Russell Freedman
A Dream of Freedom, The Civil Rights Movement from 1954 to 1968 by Diane McWorther
Free at Last! Stories and Songs of Emancipation by Coreen Rappaport
Brown Girl Dreaming by Jacqueline Wood

Juvenile fiction

Revolution by Deborah Wiles
Glory Be by Augusta Scattergood
The Watsons Go to Birmingham by Christopher Paul Curtis
Walking to the Bus Rider Blues by Harriett Gillem Robinet

Postscript

Related links:

Dr. Ernst Borinski

www.pbs.org/itvs/fromswastikatojimcrow/story.html
www.tougaloo.edu/give-today/civil-rights-endowed-chair

Coe College

www.coe.edu/academics/offcampus

39594364R00048

Made in the USA
San Bernardino, CA
29 September 2016